By Rebecca Wilson Schwengber

Illustrated by Katrin Haerterich

Copyright © 2017 Language Sprout Publishing, L.L.C.
ISBN: 978-1-63354-015-6
All rights reserved. Published in the United States by Language Sprout.

languagesprout.com

One to One Giving

Language Sprout envisions a world in which every child is equipped with multilingualism.

For each Language Sprout Book you purchase, we will give one to a child in need.

Research has shown how important access to books is in a child's development.
For many around the world, books are inaccessible.
With your help, we are partnering with schools around the globe to provide colorful books to kids in need.
Thank you. Together we can change the world.

To find out more and to
Join the Language Revolution™, please check out our website.

www.LanguageSprout.com

黑色

三角形

①

紫色

圆形

红色

八边形

⑤

帮Shazam找到红色的八边形。

一共有几个？

蓝色

正方形

黄色

⑨

橘色

六边形

粉红色

心形

绿色

椭圆形

天蓝色

五角星

咖啡色

长方形

白色

菱形

帮Shazam找到白色的菱形。一共有几个?

灰色

月牙形

帮Marta找到灰色的月牙形。

一 二 三 四 五

十一 十二 十三 十四 十五

Visit us soon in our next book…

我们有宠物！

www.ingramcontent.com/pod-product-compliance
Lightning Source LLC
Chambersburg PA
CBHW080444090526
44586CB00047B/2495